How To Create And Build A Se7en Figure Government Contracting Empire!

Top ten things you need to do right now to succeed

Steven Iones

Copyright © 2021 by Steven Jones

All rights reserved. This book or any portion thereof may not be reproduced or used in any manner whatsoever without the express written permission of the publisher except for the use of brief quotations in a book review.

Printed in the United States of America

First Printing, 2021

Paperback ISBN; 978 627 7505 22 6

Table of Contents

Government Contractor: What is a Government Contractor? 1
    US is little different to rest of the world 2
    Why do we choose to be a Government Contractor? 4

Government Contracting Terminologies 6
    Bid: What do we ask for? 6
    Invitation to Bid: What is an Invitation to Bid? 7
    Bidder Conference: What is a bidder Conference? 8
    Competitive bidding: What is competitive bidding? 10
    Contract: What is a Contract? 12
    Contract Amendment: What is a Contract Amendment? 13
    Government Proposal: What is a Government Proposal? 14

How to begin getting Government Contracts 16
    Most Commonly Asked Questions 20

Finding contract opportunities 23
    Contract teaming 24

How to Register for Government Contracts 29

How to Qualify for Government Contracts 35

How to Get Government Contracts: Prepare Your Proposal 37

How to Win a Government IT Contract 44

DARPA's commitment to small businesses 54

Small Business Designation 57

How to do marketing of your government contracting business 60

Expert Insight 68

Future opportunities 74

Government Contractor: What is a Government Contractor?

A government contractor is a private firm that manufactures and provides goods and services for government entities. Contractors are hired by the government when they win contracts that are there to bid. Government contractors can obtain contracts by responding to proposals with the lowest cost bid required by law. Government contractors, like government organizations, exist in a variety of sizes. Larger firms will seek government contracts for tens of millions of dollars. These larger businesses are often interested in bidding on federal projects, but they are also interested in state and municipal contracts. Smaller businesses are more likely to seek more minor agreements, more closely aligned with their company skills and scope of work. Smaller companies will seek out state and municipal contracts since they have fewer resources. So, how do you get started as a federal contractor? Depending on the state in where the firm is based, the process may vary. For becoming a registered vendor, each state has its own set of rules and regulations. Therefore the first step is to contact your state, county, or local procurement office. Once you've registered as a vendor, it's just a question of knowing when a government contract is available. The government advertises what they intend to buy for most transactions above $25,000, and the bidding is open to the public. If you come across a perfectly up to your alley project, submit your most acceptable bids and give it a go. While several procedural aspects to consider, getting your foot in the door is the most critical initial step.

US is little different to rest of the world

Every year, the US government buys a startling amount of goods and services. Many small firms want to offer their products or services to the government. Fortunately, small businesses wanting to conduct business with the government at the local, state, federal, and international levels are legally obligated to get a substantial portion of the billions in annual contracts. So, why aren't all tiny firms utilizing government contracts? Because winning government contracts isn't simple, and most business owners don't know how to accomplish it. To begin with, the government needs small company owners to pass a stringent qualifying procedure.

However, after you've met the requirements, you'll be eligible for a slice of the billiondollar pie. There are procedures to follow and requirements to satisfy firms looking to get their foot in the door to win a contract bid. First, do your homework to learn about the federal marketplace and how the target agency chooses to buy items. It will assist you in creating your bid. Although pricing is important, so are prior performance, experience, and the stability of the firm. You may be requested to deliver an oral presentation once you submit your proposal. When the agency has limited the field to two or three bids, this is likely to happen. You might get in touch frequently for further information during the government procurement process. Well, it is excellent news since it indicates that they are interested. Overall, the most challenging aspects of getting a government contract are studying the market and writing an error-free proposal.

Municipal and state governments and federal organizations in the United States enable businesses of all sizes and sorts to compete for government contracts. Typically, these contracts are for goods and services, as well as technical support and research. If your company successfully obtains a government contract, it may augment present cash sources, improve your reputation, and raise your chances of getting future agreements.

Even though multimillion-dollar federal government contracts granted to giant corporations receive the most of the publicity, don't allow this to deter you from selling to the government. Small enterprises have lots of opportunities as well. Government agencies may order everything from town vehicles to paper towels at any moment. The goal is to make sure you have what the government needs and to get the contract. In the approaching quarter, your state government, for example, may be seeking leather office chairs. You offer office equipment as a small firm, but you must fulfill the bid specifications before you bid on the contract. You will waste your time bidding on this contract if the state needs leather chairs and you only supply or make nylon chairs. The government may occasionally propose a contract for a service, such as the destruction of secret records. Bids for information technology, technical support, intellectual property, or research on a new product design may also be requested by the government. Small companies are required by law to get a high amount of government contracts, so it's critical to grasp the rules for making bids, as well as what the government considers to be a "small business."

Why do we choose to be a Government Contractor?

Contracting with the government has a lot of advantages. It might not be the most successful business, but it could give you an opportunity that other buyers would not be able to supply: This client pays you regularly. Government contracting gives firms, tiny and medium-sized enterprises, access to a plethora of lucrative, long-term contracts. Many federal government contracts, for example, have three to five-year contract periods. This ensures a consistent cash flow over time with reasonable profit margins.

Government contracts can help your company expand quickly. Companies now active in government contracting began with modest arrangements and progressed to larger and larger contracts. Start preparing your business for long-term development in the Federal Government sector today. The government is actively looking for vendors in every industry. The government is interested in any service or product your firm offers.

Government Contracting Terminologies

First and foremost, you will hear these terms frequently when you begin your career as a government contractor. It would be ideal if you joined in as well. Otherwise, it will be difficult.

Bid: What do we ask for?

An invitation is a solicitation, request, or quotation to respond to a government and contractual agreement. According to the law, government agencies must open tenders when seeking treatment or other services. A well-known principle to avoid "betting inside," the company will obtain a nondisclosure agreement. This is beneficial to private government organizations because it creates competition and thus reduces prices. There are many types of advertisements, including RFI, RFP, RFQ, and ITB.

How do people make more money? Since it is in a public place, it seems easy to find this. But because many government agencies adopt different methods, finding these methods can be difficult and time-consuming. This is where FindRFP starts.

A government contract, bid, or RFP lists sales and services are from state government contractors. The US government is one of the largest consumers of goods and services in the United States. If you want to win a partnership with the government response, you need to understand how the alliance organization provides and delivers.

The government signs an agreement with the state government through the General Services Administration (GSA). GSA uses contract equipment to purchase goods and services that are valuable to government agencies.

The sales and services purchased by GSA range from cleaning and catering services to IT, telecommunications, and contracts. Most GSA agreements are for sales and equipment-related services, including bulk materials, equipment and services, construction, repair and maintenance, information technology and online services, office and other sales (purchase or lease), and all government agency vehicles (Buy or lease).

GSA promotes government cooperation and donations with other countries and other regions of the world. GSA enables small, HUBZone women-owned (formerly non-commercial) businesses, veterans, and former businesses with disabilities. Some small companies have also "neglected." According to the agreement, some agreements are reserved for competition among small or disadvantaged enterprises.

Invitation to Bid: What is an Invitation to Bid?

An invitation to bid, also known as a sealed bid or invitation for bid, is a request for contractors to submit proposals for a project involving a specific product or service.. It is usually used for more than $100,000. Although ITB is very similar to RFP (Request Request), it focuses more on price than project ideas. As with any other type of business, invitations are usually issued to contractors who offer meager costs. But remember, this is not always the case—other things to consider, such as the type of sales or skills needed to complete the job.

So how does the supplier know if the bid is RFP, RFQ, RFI, or ITB? In most cases, advertising agencies will show this on their pages or portals. If not, they will be listed in the promotional letter, especially in the title or first paragraph. There are several types of trees because knowing the diversity of each form helps determine whether the activity is suitable for you and whether it is worthwhile in the end.

Bidder Conference: What is a bidder Conference?

The bidder's meeting is a meeting arranged by the institution when issuing a new bid proposal. The bidder meeting is designed to allow interested and qualified suppliers to raise questions about the project. This will enable suppliers to understand better whether their company is interested in looking for the project and whether it is qualified to complete the work.

Usually, the bidder meeting will be arranged shortly after the proposal is released. How long after the publication date the bidders' meeting is held depends entirely on the duration of the submission period. Contracts with a short turnaround time are usually scheduled on the first day of the conference announcement. Sometimes, these contracts have no bidder meetings at all. The contractor needs to read through the specifications of each bidder to determine whether to hold a bidder meeting.

For bids that are open for one month or longer, the bidders' meeting is usually held within one or two weeks of the issue date. Bidder meetings, also known as pre-proposal meetings, are generally held where the project work will take place. In addition to answering questions from potential bidders, the pre-proposal meeting will also allow bidders to visit the worksite. The bidder's conference sometimes includes a site visit by the project manager.

When it comes to bidder meetings, each meeting will vary from contract to contract. It should be noted that some pre-proposal meetings will be mandatory, while others will be optional. When reading through the bid specifications, bidders will immediately understand this. If a bidder meeting is required, it will be marked as "mandatory" in the document. If the meeting is not mandatory, it will usually be designated as "optional" or "non-mandatory." That being said, it is essential to remember that bidder meetings are a great way to establish reports with government agencies and an excellent way for you to get involved.

Competitive bidding: What is competitive bidding?

Competitive bidding is a public bidding process whose purpose is to allow companies to put together their best proposals and compete for specific projects. According to the law, every government agency that issues bids needs to perform this process. Competitive bidding creates an open, fair and transparent environment. This effectively implies that any firm, regardless of its size, yearly revenue, or other comparable characteristics, will be welcomed into the bidding process and have equal access to the same possibilities as other rivals.

Competitive bidding is beneficial to companies competing for projects and government agencies that release projects. By creating a competitive environment, agencies can keep costs low and attract the most qualified companies to do the job. Government agencies frequently conduct bidding as a reverse auction, in which the buyer and seller roles are reversed. In a reverse auction, bids begin at a fixed amount and gradually fall dependent on the number of submissions received.

This process will continue until the end of the public bidding period. The company with the best offer or price wins the contract to perform the work or supply the product. The bid deadline is a specific date (usually a specific time) when bids are closed to the public to submit requests. At this time, only submitted proposals will be considered eligible. The deadline is an integral part of the bidding process because it creates a level playing field for contractors to write and offer the best proposals for the project at hand. It is also essential to establish it from the beginning because most (if not all) contracts have a specific start date and time frame for the completion of the project. This ensures that the work will be completed on time.

As many contractors know, the deadline for each bid varies from project to project. Proposals can be open for submission at any time between one day and two days to several months. If the contract's turnaround date is short, the agency is likely to need products or services urgently. Usually, these contracts will be labeled "emergency contracts," or the agency will indicate that it has a short turnaround time. However, under normal circumstances, the agreement will be open for at least one week. FindRFP has a 24-hour turnaround time, which essentially means that any bids sent today will be emailed to you tomorrow morning. The 24-hour turnaround time ensures that FindRFP provides you with the most complete, accurate, and timely RFP. The bid also includes deadlines for various other matters, such as bidder issues, declarations of interest, and bidder awards. Please pay close attention to the deadline to ensure that your well-designed proposal will not be rejected.

Closing Date:-deadline for all bid submissions

Change of contract — extension, termination, adjustment, or modification of the contract Contractor — a person who signs a contract to perform a service or offers items in a contract Comparative value reflects the corresponding cost of the contract.

Acquisition - the process of acquiring equipment or services, including knowing the requirements and purchasing from the goods for sale or from the sale

The purpose is to get a response to a co-operative request, which is a response to a problem, necessity, or purpose of the request

Bid (IFB, IFB) -IFB is also called a closed bid. It usually costs more than $ 100,000, it's a competition, and those who want to get the lowest will win.

Hearing Request (RFP, RFP) or Inquiry Request (RFT, RFT) - Although RFP is used for a fee of US $ 25,000 or more, it is used for lower prices which cannot be selected based on these requirements. The RFP is used to obtain a cost-effective solution based on the monitoring methods found in the RFP.

Quotation Request (RFQ, RFQ) -When the cost of goods and services is less than $ 25,000 received, an RFQ is provided. Keep marketing documents easily so that the agreement can be obtained quickly.

Contract: What is a Contract?

The agreement is the responsibility between the two parties to agree to adhere to the rules already established. Because it is about a government contract, an agreement is established between the government agency and the builder or the company that wants to do business. The contract is shown after the return period, and the board announces the name of the successful contractor. Like most contracts, an advertising contract contains information that a contractor must fulfill to perform the contract. These can include but are not limited to the exact name of the business users, the project's expiration date, the terms of the agreement, and much more. Each relationship is different, so you must read it to understand and meet all expectations. This will ensure and help maintain good relations with government agencies and pave the way for future rewards.

Contract Amendment: What is a Contract Amendment?

Subsidiary changes are the addition, reduction, modification, or change of existing ideas intended to be sold. Contract changes, also known as contract supplements or renewable agreements, are provided within days, weeks, or even months after the first business is provided. Whether the amendment has been approved depends on the existing contract. Some bids will have a lot of changes, while others will not.

What is involved in changing the contract? The following are examples of changes that may be made:

- Change the last date for this request
- Change the activity
- Questions and answers on sales difficulties
- Changes in agreement style

Acquisition - the process of acquiring equipment or services, including knowing the requirements and purchasing from the goods for sale or from the sale

The purpose is to get a response to a co-operative request, which is a response to a problem, necessity, or purpose of the request

Bid (IFB, IFB) -IFB is also called a closed bid. It usually costs more than $ 100,000, it's a competition, and those who want to get the lowest will win.

Hearing Request (RFP, RFP) or Inquiry Request (RFT, RFT) - Although RFP is used for a fee of US $ 25,000 or more, it is used for lower prices which cannot be selected based on these requirements. The RFP is used to obtain a cost-effective solution based on the monitoring methods found in the RFP.

Quotation Request (RFQ, RFQ) -When the cost of goods and services is less than $ 25,000 received, an RFQ is provided. Keep marketing documents easily so that the agreement can be obtained quickly.

Contract: What is a Contract?

The agreement is the responsibility between the two parties to agree to adhere to the rules already established. Because it is about a government contract, an agreement is established between the government agency and the builder or the company that wants to do business. The contract is shown after the return period, and the board announces the name of the successful contractor. Like most contracts, an advertising contract contains information that a contractor must fulfill to perform the contract. These can include but are not limited to the exact name of the business users, the project's expiration date, the terms of the agreement, and much more. Each relationship is different, so you must read it to understand and meet all expectations. This will ensure and help maintain good relations with government agencies and pave the way for future rewards.

Contract Amendment: What is a Contract Amendment?

Subsidiary changes are the addition, reduction, modification, or change of existing ideas intended to be sold. Contract changes, also known as contract supplements or renewable agreements, are provided within days, weeks, or even months after the first business is provided. Whether the amendment has been approved depends on the existing contract. Some bids will have a lot of changes, while others will not.

What is involved in changing the contract? The following are examples of changes that may be made:

- Change the last date for this request
- Change the activity
- Questions and answers on sales difficulties
- Changes in agreement style

- In addition to pre-scheduled meetings updates, government agencies do not always provide information to anyone.

It is usually only provided to interested sellers who have shown interest in the institution that issued the item. To ensure that you are notified of any changes, it is best to contact the service organization and show interest. In addition, if FindRFP sends you the first price and the institution has a link form on its page for you to fill out, it is best to fill out the form. By doing this, you will be added to the supplier list, and you will be notified of any changes to the service.

Government Proposal: What is a Government Proposal?

The intent/proposals of the government, sometimes called an intergovernmental agreement, is a response written by a listed company to a government agency to purchase goods or services. If an organization needs a project or service, it can issue a government RFP at any time. They do this in public so that the work can be done fairly and at a lower cost.

Federal acquisition regulations govern all public opinion, and most public agencies have similar rules and regulations. According to the FAR, the request includes details, how the appeal should be processed? And the procedures used for the review. Therefore, government opinions are often sufficient to satisfy all requirements.

The shortest government interview is usually five to ten pages, and the main idea is hundreds of pages of details.

How to begin getting Government Contracts

Establishing a company to supply goods and services to government entities necessitates regular yet exact filings, adherence to federal and state rules, and accurate financial data. To work as a government contractor, you must follow a set of strict guidelines.

Small companies are an essential element of the American economy. The government acknowledges this by spending more than $4 trillion every year with large and small firms, with over $440 billion going to small enterprises alone. As a result, if you desire to go through the procedure and operate within the regulations for selling goods and services to the US government, it's a big market worth pursuing. There's a source of fresh income prospects that far too few tiny company owners notice in their hunt for improved small business finance and new client opportunities: the US government. The federal government is a massive corporation that, like any other company, requires the acquisition of products and services to run correctly.

You may be one of those suppliers thanks to government contracts for small enterprises federal government frequently contracts firms of all sizes for anything from military vehicles and equipment to paper clips and Post-its. If you sell to businesses or nonprofits, there's a high chance you'll be able to sell your services to government entities as well. Despite these advantages, even small company owners aware of government contracting prospects avoid applying for government contracts for various reasons. The most common of which is that they find the procedure frightening.

Let's dig in to explain why you should put your worries aside and look for government contracts for small enterprises. Then we'll teach you how to discover government contracts that are up for bid and put together an application that gives you the best chance of winning the proposal for the job.

The first step is to determine what you want to market using the North American Industry Classification System (NAICS) codes (NAICS).

The North American Industry Classification Systems Association's website has a list of such codes. The codes are used to categorize a company's economic sector, industry, and nation. Keep in mind that, depending on your product or service capabilities, you may require multiple NAICS numbers, so examine carefully. One of the first things the government will look at to verify your eligibility as a federal contractor is your NAICS code; contracts aren't issued without one.

Apply for a free Dun & Bradstreet DUNS Number – a nine-digit identifying number for each company's physical location – and an Open Ratings Past Performance Evaluation.

These assessments are based on a statistical analysis of performance data and survey answers and a rating based on an independent audit of customer references.

Register with the System for Award Management (SAM) website, the federal government's central database of suppliers doing business with it, after having your NAICS codes and DUNS number.

According to the Small Business Administration, the Federal Acquisitions Regulation (FAR) system requires all potential suppliers to be registered in SAM before a contract is given or a purchase agreement is executed.

You will be issued a Commercial and Government Entity (CAGE) code when you register with SAM, which you may be asked for when responding to solicitations.

Small companies seeking federal contracts will need to get the following in addition to a NAICS code and DUNS number to assist and identify their business, industry, and product categories:

For tax purposes, you'll need a Federal Employer Identification Number (FEIN), a Standard Industrial Classification (SIC) code, Product and Service Codes (PSC), and Federal Supply Class Codes (FSC).

"Set-aside" contracts obtaining a minor business set-aside designation might also provide your firm with an advantage over the competition.

Woman-owned, disadvantaged-owned, service-disabled-veteran–owned, and HUBZone small companies are among the set-aside categories. "Set aside" indicates that the contract must be awarded to a small firm with one of those certificates, barring large businesses from responding to the solicitation with proposals or bids.

A "sole-source award" occurs, in which a contract is granted to a qualified business without going through the competitive procedure.

Each fiscal year, the federal government sets explicit targets for granting contracts to small firms.

- Small firms will receive 23 percent of prime contracts, according to the government.
- Women-owned small companies receive 5% of prime and subcontracts.
- Small disadvantaged firms receive 5% of prime and subcontracts.
- HUBZone small companies receive 5% of prime and subcontracts.
- Service-disabled veteran-owned small companies receive 3% of prime and subcontracts.

According to Lourdes Martin-Rosa, president of Government Business Solutions and a government contracting adviser for American Express OPEN, businesses may do many things to prepare themselves for success in the government contracting sector if they are dedicated.

"The Small Business Administration (SBA) is mandating procurement forecasts for government agencies," Martin-Rosa told Business News Daily, "allowing small businesses to see how much money is going to be spent by division, by quarter whom the contracting officer may be and if the contracts going to be set aside for any particular certification." Small firms will benefit from this since owners, and company development professionals will contact and ask questions, which would not be possible once a solicitation has been issued.

Most Commonly Asked Questions

1. **What constitutes a small firm for the purposes of government contracts?**

You must fulfill the Small Business Administration's size requirements for federal contracts to be considered a small business. A small firm (non-manufacturing) is defined as one that earns less than $7.5 million per year and employs fewer than 500 people (manufacturing).

2. **Where can I locate government contracts for small businesses?**

SAM.gov is the most incredible place to look for federal contracts for small companies. You may also use bid-matching services or market to agencies directly.

3. **What kinds of companies are awarded government contracts?**

Many types of businesses, including small businesses, are eligible for government contracts.

4. **What is the best way to establish a small federal contracting company?**

To begin bidding on government contracts, you'll need first to create and register your firm, then apply for a DUNS Number, check for your company's NAICS code, write in the System for Award Management, and then start looking for government contracts to bid on.

What Are the Basic Steps You Must Take to Get a Government Contract?

According to the US Small Business Administration, federal government departments engage contractors to supply billions of dollars in services and products.

Small companies, as defined by SBA rules, get a large portion of government contracts. After establishing that your company satisfies the size requirements for set-aside programs, you must complete a few easy procedures to register for and begin bidding on government contracts.

Finding contract opportunities

Once you have all of your codes and any necessary set-aside certifications, you may start exploring contracting opportunities on the government's website, www.fbo.gov, once you have all of your principles and any necessary set-aside certificates (Federal Biz).

Registration is free, and you can also sign up for email alerts.

Enter your NAICS code into the site's search feature to locate contract solicitations that your company could be eligible for and that you're interested in pursuing.

Scrutinize each solicitation.

While applicable solicitations may include one or all of your NAICS numbers, there may be other limitations.

Such a solicitation may, for example, be set aside for an 8(a) contractor who must apply for and receive special certification.

Your bid will not be evaluated if you are not an 8(a) contractor, even if you have the most excellent price or value.

Prepare and submit your bid or proposal when you find an opportunity you desire.

Each solicitation will provide thorough instructions on what should be included in the proposal, how to put it together, and how to submit it (electronic or hard copy by mail).

Make sure you follow the directions to the letter.

Noncompliant applications will be disqualified from the start of the review process by government processors.

Martin-Rosa advises small companies to keep an eye on Sources Sought and Request for Information (RFI) postings on Federal Biz and reply to them.

Though the process takes time, she believes that the capacity to discover, investigate, and debate contractual prospects is crucial.

With a Sources Sought or RFI publication, what the government wants to see is if they can set it away in some way, Martin-Rosa added.

"Don't be scared to contact and ask questions of the contracting officer.

Contract teaming

If bidding on your own sounds intimidating, seek that opportunity on the list of interested merchants.

Martin-Rosa advises small businesses to reach out to other small or large firms to see if they might work together on a contract.

Working with companies that currently handle federal contracts can help a small firm get a leg up on the competition.

You may learn about satisfying contract criteria, completing internal and behind-the-scenes processes to meet standards and regulations, and developing a previous performance portfolio to improve your capacity to pursue contracts on your own in the future.

Finding a partner who is an extension of your firm in honesty and quality is the key to successful teaming collaborations," Martin-Rosa said.

"Small firms have as much, if not more, knowledge than giant corporations.

You have to provide it to the federal government at a meager cost.

There are measures you may take in addition to registering on SAMS to find federal contracting opportunities that are a good fit for your company's goods or services.

The following are the effective methods for locating government contracts forbid:

Navigate SAM.gov.

SAM.gov is the federal contracting website to go to if you're looking for a contract for $25,000 or more.

You may also look at contracts that have already been granted, which may help you prepare future offers.

Seek a subcontracting opportunity.

While the SAM.gov database deals with direct contracts with government agencies (known as prime contracts in official speak), small companies can look into another type of government contract:

subcontracting. Subcontracting possibilities, as the name indicates, entail negotiating contracts with current government contractors to execute a portion of the work assigned by prime contractors. Subcontractors, in other words, are the vendor's vendors. Subcontracting on government contracts may be a lucrative business opportunity and an opportunity to learn more about government contracting before bidding on prime contracts with the US government.

The SBA offers a searchable database called SUB.

Net that emphasizes available subcontracting opportunities, similar to SAM.gov.

Searching SUB-Net for subcontracting opportunities is a fantastic place to start if you're new to government contracting or want to add a layer of experience between government agency clients and your own company.

Market directly to agencies.

You can advertise your small company directly to either targeted agencies or prime contractors if you're in a very specialized industry or know exactly which government agency your small business is best suited to contract with.

To do so, you'd use SAM.gov and SUB-Net to look for current procurement requirements. Then you may explain to those agencies why your firm is the best candidate for the job.

Procurement conferences, business gatherings, and even contract matchmaking events provide opportunities to network with agency decision-makers.

Work with a bid-matching service.

Subscribing to a bid-matching service can be a beneficial way to get government contracts for small firms with more comprehensive services unclear about their perfect government agency fit. Although most local Procurement Technical Assistance Centers provide free bid-matching services, you may also pay for private, more specialized services.

Working with a bid-matching firm also provides experienced government contracting mentors who can assist you with the proposal and procurement process.

By registering with SAM, you make your company visible to contractors looking for work. The Small Business Administration (SBA) provides a list of programs and tools for getting government contracts. Look for current possibilities on different websites, such as the FedBizOpps website, which publishes all announcements for federal contracts for $25,000 or more. The GSA Schedules Program, which might find on the General Services Administration's website, includes current supply and service contracting opportunities and information regarding the agency's smallbusiness set aside program. To apply for or bid on contracts, follow the requirements in the announcements or solicitations.

How to Register for Government Contracts

Let's speak about how to get started with government contracting now that you've been convinced of the importance of government contracts for small businesses.

As you might expect, a few more procedures are required to become a contractual vendor for the US government, one of which is enrolling in the System for Award Management. Here's how to sign up:

Obtain your DUNS number.

Before applying for government contracts, you must first get a Dun & Bradstreet DUNS Number for each of your company's physical locations.

Using the online DUNS Request Service, you can get a DUNS Number for free.

Find your company's NAICS code.

Most firms also require a North American Industry Classification System (NAICS) code, which defines your company's industry, nation, and economic sector for government contracting reasons. This code is required to register your company. For help determining your industry code, contact the Small Business Administration (SBA).

Keep in mind that if your company works in numerous industries or sectors, you may need to submit multiple NAICS numbers.

Determine your business size.

You might think that selecting your company doesn't need much consideration.

However, to be eligible for federal contracts for small companies, you must meet the SBA's size requirements.

The SBA has a Size Standards Tool to assist you in quickly answer this issue. It utilizes your NAICS number and other basic information about your firm to assess if it qualifies as an SBAdesignated small business.

Register in the System for Award Management (SAM)

The US government maintains the System for Award Management (SAM), a database of firms interested in federal contracts. Unlike a private sector business client who may find your company on Google, LinkedIn, or another search or social network, government decision-makers utilize SAM to find possible providers.

As a result, small companies seeking government contracts should devote the same amount of time and attention to developing a compelling and search-friendly SAM profile as they would to developing an SEO strategy or updating your company's LinkedIn page. To get started, you'll need to register with the SAM system as a government vendor. While your SAM profile must be updated at least once a year to be active, companies who are serious about winning federal contracts should update and enhance their SAM profile at least quarterly, if not monthly, or more frequently. • Creating your small business profile: Begin by registering for the site and conducting a few searches for firms comparable to yours to see what information they put in their profiles. The keywords you use are crucial, just as they are in traditional search engine optimization. However, keep in mind that the services you provide to government customers may differ from those you provide to private sector customers, which means your search keywords may also alter.

- ❖ Creating your capability statement: The capability statement for your company is arguably the essential part of your SAM profile.

This is the government's equivalent of your elevator pitch—your chance to describe what your company does in a few sentences and how your product or service may help government clients. Although you're selling to government entities, keep in mind that the decision-makers within those agencies are actual people.

Avoid the temptation to describe your products or services in too technical or bureaucratic terms.

Working with a government agency doesn't mean you have to hide your brand's individuality!

5. Solicit past performance evaluations.

If you're new to bidding on government contracts, an Open Ratings Inc. past performance evaluation may be helpful—although it is not mandatory.

This impartial auditing and grading system, performed by a private sector of the Dun & Bradstreet Co., analyses survey responses from your former customers to generate a numerical rating of your prior performance.

- Contact the business department or the secretary of state's office in your state, which is usually responsible for submitting corporation paperwork.
- Obtain the assistance of a reputable business or legal advisor.

You might want a professional opinion on other organizational forms, such as a sole proprietorship, a limited liability company, a corporation, or other structures that are appropriate for your firm. File the required paperwork to get a municipal occupational license, depending on the type of company product or service.

For advice on bonding and personal or professional liability coverage, contact your insurance agent.

1. Conduct research to aid in the creation of a business strategy. Experienced personnel, volunteers, and other resources from the US Small Business Administration and SCORE can help new business owners prepare efficient

business plans. Universities with wellregarded schools fund business incubators dedicated solely to entrepreneurs who want to sell their products and services to federal and state government agencies.

2. Create your business strategy, if necessary, using a template.

Gather information like owner credentials, financial documents, and marketing and feasibility study results. If you are seeking finance for your government contracting firm from a financial institution, a private investor, or a venture capitalist, your business plan is the most crucial stage. It must be compelling enough to distinguish your company from others seeking investment.

1. To register a company that wants to bid on government contracts, go to bpn.gov/ccr. When you register for the CCR database, have your DUNS and EIN or TIN numbers ready. Your company information is visible to agency officials and contracting officers once you complete your CCR registration.

Potential government contractors must also provide other information, such as industry codes and contact information for the owners.

Every day, the Federal Business Opportunities website, Fedbizopps.gov or FBO.gov, posts new federal contracting opportunities.

Establish ties with other government contractors, particularly prime contractors,

1. Frequently seek out small businesses or newly created government contracting firms for joint ventures on large projects. Contractor contact information can be found on the FBO website or in the CCR database. Participate in government-sponsored outreach events. Every federal government department maintains an outreach office committed to meeting the requirements of businesses interested in selling goods and services to the government. To encourage networking among government contractors, outreach offices hold seminars, meet-andgreet events, and other events.

How to Qualify for Government Contracts

Every year, the US government spends hundreds of millions of dollars on contracts with private businesses. Uncle Sam is, in reality, the country's most significant buyer of products and services. To compete for federal contracts, you must first register your company with the US government's unified contractor database.

1. The IRS will provide you with an employer identification number. You may apply for an EIN for free online and get it straight away. A tax identification number, or TIN, is another name for the EIN.

2. Obtain a DUNS number from Dun & Bradstreet. This is a globally recognized company identification number that is necessary for bidding on federal contracts. Registration is free and may be done over the phone. Your DUNS number will be sent to you right away.

3. Visit the webpage for the Central Contractor Registration. To begin the registration procedure, click "Start New Registration."

4. Enter your identifying details and click "Create a User Account." Proceed to the following steps of the registration

by answering five security questions (e.g., "mother's maiden name").

5. Give information about your company, including your EIN and DUNS numbers. Your NAICS industry classification code must also be provided. If you don't know your NAICS code, you may look it up using the CCR website's online tools by entering terms that characterize your company.

6. After completing the application, you should get an email confirmation of your registration within three to five business days. You can bid on government contracts once you've registered.

How to Get Government Contracts: Prepare Your Proposal

Even if you've written proposals and scopes of work orders for potential clients in the private sector, nothing compares to the unique process of drafting a government contract proposal. In reality, submitting a bid or submission to a government body may be more comparable to filing your business taxes or filling out a stack of DMV papers. Even yet, as long as you stay within the boundaries of agency processes and expectations, there are plenty of possibilities to convey your unique value add and let your company shine inside the pages of your proposal.

1. Understand the solicitation type.

There are several different ways for government organizations to solicit bids from potential government contractors, and each has its jargony nomenclature and paperwork breakdown, as you might imagine.

However, the style of solicitation used for a specific contract might reveal a lot about what the agency wants from your proposal, so it's crucial to know the difference.

The following are the three most common types of government contracting solicitations you'll find on SAM.gov or anywhere else that list government contracting opportunities.

Request for Quotation (RFQ)

For government organizations, a request for quotation is a streamlined procurement method that is generally utilized for contracts under $150,000.

While this is deemed simple by government standards, it may be more extensive than the previous scope of work proposals your company has produced for private companies.

View prior RFQ proposals in the SAM.gov database to understand better how an RFQ should be performed effectively for a company in your sector.

Request for Proposal (RFP)

Requests for proposals are used for more extensive negotiated acquisitions, allowing for some back-and-forth between the government agency and the potential vendor to reach a mutually acceptable pricing and conditions agreement. The process begins when a government agency releases an RFP outlining the contract's criteria, standard terms and conditions, and the material that bidders must provide as part of their proposal.

When responding to a request for proposal, having complete and correct information is critical, so if you're unsure how to reply to specific elements in an RFP, contact the contracting officer for clarification before submitting your proposal.

Invitation for Bid (IFB)

Invitations for bids are secret solicitation processes for government procurement in which the agency and the vendor do not negotiate.

The bid package that has been filed is deemed final, and the price point is typically viewed as the most crucial distinction between qualified bidders.

Because of the sealed and final nature of the bidding procedure, responding to an IFB may be the instance where you'll want to be extra cautious while filling out your paperwork and determining your pricing the first time.

There will be no time for discussion or amendments, so if you overshoot the bid or leave out critical information, the agency will almost definitely reject your offer and award the contract to someone else.

Follow the uniform contract format.

Regardless of their kind, all solicitations have the same expectation that prospective contractors follow a particular pattern.

The ability to follow guidelines in the proposal formatting and submission procedure is just as important as the content of your proposal in obtaining government contracts.

As a result, make sure you follow all of the schedules and forms in the solicitation in the specified order, structure, and time.

The SBA's free online course "Government Contracting 101" is an excellent resource for learning more about the purpose, forms, and expectations of each Uniform Contract Format's ten parts.

Price your bid appropriately.

Before issuing a proposal request, federal contracting officers must verify that goods and services for government agencies are acquired at fair and reasonable rates. They do extensive market research to determine regular pricing.

At the same time, most solicitations receive a large number of competing bids, presenting you, the business owner, with the difficult challenge of making a competitive offer while still maximizing your profit potential.

As you might expect, getting your contract price right is crucial to winning successful government contracts.

You must evaluate your expenses throughout the bidding process and during contract fulfillment while leaving adequate room for day-to-day overhead. When bidding, consider that contracting officers aren't looking for the lowest price but rather the best overall value.

To increase your company's attractiveness as the "best value" offer, look for methods to add value to your proposal without raising overhead expenses.

Additional Resources for Government Contracts

We hope this primer on how to get government contracts for small businesses has been helpful, but there's always more to learn in this vast and complex sector. Fortunately, theSmall Company Administration (SBA) and other government agencies have made considerable efforts to provide helpful information for small business owners interested in federal contracts. We've compiled a list of some of the most valuable resources.

SBA Government Contracting Classroom

Do you want to have a better grasp of government contracting before entering the federal market? The Small Business Administration's Federal Contracting Classroom is a fantastic online course series that covers all you need to know about government contracts for small businesses. These classes are an excellent way to learn more about the precise paperwork and procedures involved in registering for, locating, and obtaining government contracts for small companies.

Procurement Center Representatives

If you'd prefer to learn more about federal contracting possibilities in person, contact your local SBA Procurement Center Representative (PCR).

Procurement representatives provide aspiring government contractors with training, mentorship, and counseling, as well as in-person matchmaking events between agencies and qualifying small companies.

Here's how to locate a PCR near you.

GSA or SBA Mentor-Portege Program

Mentorprotege programs are offered by the Small Business Administration and the Government

Services Administration to help to qualify small companies to interact with more experienced government contractors.

While the SBA MentorProtégé Program is only available to 8(a) development program participants, you may be qualified to join the GSA Mentor-Protégé Program without any additional company development criteria.

There's no disputing that joining the federal contracting market comes with a steep learning curve. Procuring government contracts, like everything else you've taught yourself as a small company owner, is a skill you can master. You may enter the lucrative world of government contracts for small enterprises by investing time and effort.

How to Win a Government IT Contract

Companies of all kinds in all industries often receive a large portion of their IT services from external providers. The global cost of IT outsourcing is about $ 900 billion, and the company buys IT consulting machinery integration, maintenance and repair, IT infrastructure management services, and much more. The following are some of my tips on how to ensure IT government contracts belongs to you.

- Internet access, communication, establish a communication system and understand the pain that government agencies need. Learn what makes government workers sleep through the night - or harass them every day. You need to ask yourself: 'Can I help them to solve this problem?

- Follow-up - Take time to research major topics, recent actions, legal documents, and events affecting government agencies. For example, if you have recently developed a strategy to promote cloud computing - the main goal being to increase efficiency and reduce costs - will your business or service help government agencies achieve this? How do you make sure you have to do what you want and respond to the needs?

- Safety and compliance: Customers such as the Cabinet Office and U.S. government agencies will not be easily swayed by a growing list of things. Data security is crucial for big businesses like this (government or private). Make sure you have the necessary qualifications to work, and you can ensure that you are complying with the GDPR.

- Get newsletters - Once you find your first client in a group, it is best to ask if they can do some research and give you a page. This will provide an opportunity for customers who have value-added comfort to be recognized by someone to ensure that your business or service is truly effective and has produced good visibility. Once you enter the door, your reputation will be spread.

- Save your jobs - it doesn't mean it's big enough when it comes to government. Your sales or service must be tracked to meet the requirements of government agencies. For example, in terms of IT, is your business or service meeting the suitable security measures? Can you provide the support level that users need? This helps foster a culture of interdependence that is the foundation of a partnership and initiation process.

- Provide products or services that people often use - In the end, no matter how much research you have and the network you build, if people don't like using your business or service, it's impossible. Go back to the roots and make sure you are using the right users. Give people clean and fun jobs.

- Create a balanced understanding of business outcomes: For many IT buyers and sellers, it isn't easy to reach a consensus on business objectives. More than 60% of the contractors reviewed, the group did not follow the entire negotiation process within the expected business. IT buyers experience a series of intensive internal dates with a contract and terminate the agreement with the supplier. They believe they do not have enough time for all business partners to explain the potential benefits from external IT business. Whether it is savings, increased productivity, or rapid depletion and skills. As a result, they often do not hope for the essentials of making new agreements or re-establishing existing ones. In the 100% of the contracts we reviewed, the business results were not well defined, and the leading performance indicators were insufficient; they look costly. Resultantly, it is not sufficient to measure the expected business results. Because they do not know what a business buys, a salesperson may not know how to offer talent and other things. And because suppliers need to adhere to how consumers can apply the contract and their methods, they cannot expect to find new ideas. To ensure that the goals are clear, buyers and sellers need to break downtime and meet challenges. Consumers should include endusers and business department executives in negotiating agreements with the latest providers. The desired result should be included in this low-level agreement, and it is understood that there will be some additional alliances over time. In another financial management company, IT leaders insisted on involving the CEO, other C-level executives, and board members in deciding whom to donate. Executives from large companies are invited to visit them, and the committee receives changes regularly during the election process. With this information, business owners and all other stakeholders can help the contract team set short- and long-term goals and integrate management processes.

- Emphasize the long-term: Of the contracts, we reviewed, about 80% of the work requirements were the lowest. This is necessary at some point but leaves little room for future integration. Competitive groups argue that more work needs to be done, but they do too little or too little to repay the terms. In addition, under normal circumstances, consumers have never considered the future of IT-based on any need. Almost the same part of the agreement we reviewed (80% to 90%) did not include appropriate measures to promote long-term viability. To realize the long-term vision, commitment and professional knowledge, consumers must clarify the various service requirements and quantities initially expected according to specific business goals and then use regular "horses"meetings to refine and modify the needs of service providers. Promote new ideas and find the elements to realize them. IT buyers should also give suppliers a clear understanding of the business and its key goals: What technological advancements can technology bring to help companies achieve their goals? A mutually agreed alliance can combine the constant needs and choices of both parties and change some management strategies when you provide colour, workload, or workload changes. Both groups can accept a variety of lighting environments in which they can re-enlighten and re-analyze words. Consumers can also participate in customer meetings to understand and guide long-term improvements. The home appliance subsidiary discussed the changes in IT providers because it chose the best way to adapt to the cloud design. The company does not want to upgrade existing services immediately, so it has developed a three-year transformation plan with suppliers. The promoters will continue to provide traditional services in the first year as they gradually change their work on the platform in the second and third years. Modifications are frequent, and both parties agree to adjust the pricing method accordingly. The changes are still in progress, but the buyer has made significant progress in moving work to the cloud thanks to the system.

- Follow the steps for preparation and perseverance: Approximately 75% of long-term IT contractors were screened, stating that consumers expect this relationship to lead to a dynamic IT transformation. But in most cases, there is little evidence that the way of thinking or earning the necessary funds has changed the method of experimentation. For example, 75% of contractors regard raising prices as the primary goal of the change but ignore improvement according to the destination. IT representatives, rather than business partners usually lead any discussion of ideas for change. The latter were told how they would need it. As far as they are concerned, suppliers typically do not know the roadmap plan, which is why they think they will not affect the impact of the change. In most cases, nothing is clear about the origin of the change, the project of interest, and how to get there.

- IT transformation cannot be successful without two things: working together for change, combining IT architecture options, and what we call transformation "resilience" —or severe interest in planning and action. Buyers and sellers need to create flexible design systems; growing together and developing partnerships with industry leaders is essential. Buyers and sellers need to supplement this map with a detailed plan to achieve a new application. In this way, they can create a framework for measuring the impact of any IT transformation. Sales teams can assess the cost, but they can also follow cost-effective methods (both IT and IT), such as cost-recovery and delivery time. Under this approach, IT consumers will be able to manage things effectively in IT (depending on the ideas of their business partners), and IT vendors can be confident that their financial sector will be based on reliable business cases, not a vague definition of success. The investment banking group has set targets for a radical change at the beginning of the negotiations with the buyer partner. The coalition team is working to reduce costs by 40% over the first two years and use providers' services to reduce it by another 40% over the next six years. These numbers encourage banks and IT providers. Together, they decided to adopt a more flexible approach to changing banks - for example, moving to cloud computing and removing other jobs - and establishing each one based on the ideas they had initially been made. The bank, its stakeholders, and IT providers have been able to re-establish the relationships they have worked for and work together to support the temporary transformation of technology.

- Make a successful alliance: The reality of IT procurement is that negotiations are seen as a small war in most affiliate organizations. Each party often focuses on achieving a better price rather than a merger. Instead, in most of the agreements we reviewed, trading strategies were not designed to complement each other, especially in restoring key contracts. Lowering the cost is an important goal for IT buyers, but if the customer relationship grows, this reduction will affect the value of the providers. Instead, they both have to follow the economic incentives. They can ensure that the economy is sustainable through transparency that can be used and set goals together. Instead of focusing on the price of a unit, they can also use the total value of the property on the merits. The incentives can be discussed in public in the scorecard, which follows a revenue-sharing system in the contract. Both parties also need to consider the benefits of a stable agreement, not just the initial ones. Other contracts were formed to enable one party to achieve its business and financial goals in the very first year, while the other party benefits in the years to come. We found that approximately 10% of the review contracts have incentives. The car manufacturer agreed with the IT infrastructure providers when it agreed to set a small annual budget. It also agreed to provide the necessary performance predictions for a small group of cages and hence reliable business transactions. In return, the seller offers a discount to the manufacturers and approves the revenue sharing system, and both will benefit from the change for the better. IT purchases will never end. Companies in all industries do not have the necessary control for all their IT services to be used internally. They need to rely on external suppliers to fulfil important tasks. As more and more companies try to digitalize their products and services, IT becomes more critical. Companies need to constantly review the performance of their contracts - not just to look at the technologies offered or the agreements that have been implemented, but also the skills they have acquired and the skills that have been achieved. Our research shows five ways to promote IT purchases. There may be other aspects of change. Both parties need to look at how they work in different ways — as a successful partnership; IT benefits are built together, not separately.

DARPA's commitment to small businesses

DARPA recognizes that the idea of bringing security technologies to the country often starts with the smallest. To improve the library of ideas that have been received, DARPA strongly encourages participation for all who can: industry, education, and the public.

Do your homework

Well known for the purpose and vision of DARPA, that is, to make the necessary investment in pilot technology to ensure the continued security and security of the United States. Also, highlight the travel technologies used to protect the country, which briefly describes the agency.

DARPA culture

DARPA maintains and promotes a culture of innovation and the ability to act responsibly and effectively. To that end, the council appointed high-level officials from companies, academia, and government agencies in their respective territories to deal with the current crisis and be at greater risk of violating the guidelines. The project manager (PM) is the key to working with DARPA. The PM usually works for the board for 3-5 years, and this work usually ends when the PM resigns. Looking for opportunities

DARPA-sponsored opportunities are promoted through multi-agency (BAA) announcements, research announcements (RA), or advertisements or other government-sponsored programs published on SAM.gov's official website (https://sam.gov/) and opportunities fundraiser at the Federation (www.grants.gov).

The DARPA SBIR / STTR theme is included in the DoD SBIR and STTR program announcements at https://www.dodsbirsttr.mil/submissions/login.

DARPA buys products and goods through GSA Advantage: www.gsaadvantage.gov

Attend the Next Day Meeting

The Proposer Day meeting may allow for enrollment in one-on-one discussions with DARPA project managers. Details on the applicant's date will be included in the BAA, or special notification (SN) documented at SAMbeta.gov and grants.gov.

Managing cooperation

DARPA's Contract Management Office (CMO) has the power to sign and regulate agreements, grants, contracts, and other events to achieve DARPA's R&D goal. CMO's role is to act as a procurement consultant at DARPA and award prizes in specially designated areas. The military department signs many DARPA awards on behalf of the agency, and they assist DARPA in transforming the profession into an army fighter.

For more information, please visit Contract Management.

The preferred method of submitting ideas and opinions to DARPA is to respond to one of the following funding mechanisms: to prepare or publish BAA, SBIR or STTR, RA or RFP articles. In marketing and communications, government contractors and public IT providers face some challenges.

On the one hand, the clients of federal, state, and rural decision-making clients responsible for purchasing technical and technical services - from CIOs and CTOs to project managers, IT managers, and procurement managers - represent a small group of people who are hard to reach. Adding to the problem is that government contractors must sell their products, services, and services and have a good balance between advertising and marketing activities. This means increasing awareness quickly before a contract is awarded and continuing to advertise and publicly engage for months or years from the RFP to reward — even for opposing contracts, delays, and budget crises.

Small Business Designation

To engage in small business government contracting, a company must meet specific criteria. According to SBA standards, a small business is independently owned and operated, is organized as a for-profit business, and conducts the majority of its operations in the United States, or has a company located in the United States and contributes significantly to the economy of the United States. A small firm does not have a national monopoly in its sector and can be structured legally as a partnership, sole proprietorship, or corporation. NAICS Codes

The SBA mandates that you choose the correct industry code for your company.

The North American Industry Classification System assigns different sorts of industries six-digit designations.

The NAICS page on the US Census Bureau website contains a search engine for industry categories and information to assist in determining the NAICS code that best describes your company. The Small Business Administration also provides materials and tools to assist in selecting the appropriate NAICS code.

Business Size

The SBA uses the NAICS numbers to determine the size of small companies.

The SBA's size criteria are based on the number of workers a company has had in the previous 12 months and the company's average yearly receipts for the last three years. The business owners choose the criteria that yield the most significant business size assessment. The company utilizes the size it elects to be classified as a small business by the SBA and compete on government contracting opportunities.

On its website, the Small Business Administration (SBA) gives standards for assessing business size.

DUNS Number

Businesses that do business with the federal government are required to apply for and acquire a DUNS number.

Dun & Bradstreet offers a free online registration service that provides a nine-digit number. Each of your company's physical locations will require a DUNS number.

The SBA has connections to the DUNS system, or you may go to the Dun & Bradstreet website's DUNS Request Service page.

SAM Registration

All contractors must register with the federal government's Award Management System, a database of corporations and other suppliers that deal with federal agencies. Entering your company's size is a requirement of SAM registration.

Your DUNS number, NAICS code, and employee identification number or taxpayer-identification number are also required. Although registration with SAM is not necessary for subcontractors, the SBA advises it since significant contractors and government agencies utilize it to find small companies and subcontractors.

How to do marketing of your government contracting business

Advertising for corporate decision-makers is only one part of the confusion. For small and medium-sized contractors, skills training should be extended to major contractors and large contractors to ensure fewer companies

The main contractor must also sell demand and look for young partners. They are the last and most challenging working/working class. They are market capitalists, relatives or relatives. how to navigate is the secret of success is learning

The more traffic I drop, the more likely trainees and PR routes will be in the market today.

Find pages with audiences.

Dealing with this process goes a long way for the work of a website, and the users who have used these machines-the most advanced decision makers-cannot meet the needs of those who work well. Surrounded by mountains, a single government contractor can become the backbone of buyers anywhere in their online journey.

The user is a website operator for the amount of money that a mobile phone can use for additional applications.

Audience sites are constantly changing between viewers' entrepreneurship, and the rest will use various tools to harness the power of growth, which is the same for working-class executives. For web-based listening sites, Google may suggest developing web-based listening programs in Google's main window and shooter to contain Google content and the ever-changing Google algorithm-shared content accommodation.

Combining additional costs is to share the price burden of using resources

This is not just spending money, and most people will spend it on their stomachs.

We have seen our professionals/contractors see experiments by opposing factions in the public domain. Computer and IT providers are also doing their best to "mix" those who use their tools/equipment in the company. These companies have a single component and organ, these components and organs with the development of software and the promotion of independent work Leave.

This is because it contradicts the teachings of the World Council. It also looks at how it affects interactions, which may result in costs that may be spent on mutual funds or disputes.

Create digital attractions resources for decision-makers

The website has become a natural resource for decision-makers to research projects with employees before purchasing. Paper, paper, and other materials may still help document those who make long-term decisions about the consumer's journey. Still, the size of the contractor makes them more visible in the community.

In these scenarios, the government contractor in the womb is creating a hands-on experience where electronic decay can be used as a big toe to enhance vision. These experiences should have appeared long ago. Not to be confused with the few programs that can be developed and used with 700-year-old machines compatible with analysts. Analysts also use control and digital purchases to solve the company's reaction and form a distinct Compared. The bribe starts with an answer. Highlight your skills

Government contractors have no protective measures or cannot be carried in the abdomen, stomach or intestines. Temporary organizations may not seem to have approved the use of one-hour or nondrug machines, in which case they may be better able to operate machine-made machines, which may allow them to work to improve their capabilities-or other decision-makers in court - immediately.

The fact is that you have homemade developers working on IT projects-very valuable experiments. The board of directors or the primary supervisory agency of the board of directors uses actual statistical calculation and statistical control strategies.

Write packages and in-app scripts in its annual application to take full advantage of IT equipment in the ashes of federal, state, and local governments. Multiple organizations are willing to share the first IT story, energy-saving and clothing storage in the award-winning archives, and ensure that the stars are cleaned up.

Another benefit of exploring this issue through the incentive program is to raise awareness of international and international biodiversity.

Create the events you want to sign

Contractors and IT vendors are well aware that successful corporations need very different ways of marketing and communications. Contractors and IT vendors can use these methods to connect with decision-makers to succeed in business, but money cannot say this.

Prioritization is a secret: Here are six ways business and relationships are available in the market today.

Use audience engagement pages.

Coping with curiosity is an essential aspect of the website that provides a seamless interface to the game across all user windows (in this case, government decision-makers). Government contractors and IT providers can stand in front of consumers anywhere on their online journey with listening websites.

Users who view the website anytime and anywhere via electronic devices may have the same information as sitting in the office.

Listener websites offer continuity between different viewing systems, depending on the type of tool they have used and the size of the user's window.

Listener websites are also at the forefront of search engines because Google encourages the creation of listener websites. After all, a single link for desktop and mobile websites makes it easier for Google to find Google content, and Google algorithms (invariably) share content.

Promise to publish and share group bundles through peer-to-peer activities

While doing it yourself on the idea of advertising and relationships with people allows companies to streamline events, it can also be costly and minimizes the size and complexity achieved through this partnership with business partners.

We have seen technical partners/contractors change the work of the advertising team on a variety of issues. For example, an IT consultant who provides an organization with a "conged" organization, where the business/expertise of each company is part of the fundraiser, may find that independent activities are useless.

This is because it gives decision-makers the responsibility to know how things are connected and integrate any conflicting information. Create digital campaigns to attract voters

The Internet has become an excellent way for decision-makers to research products and services before making a purchase. Sometimes a buyer's visit, paperwork, cleaning supplies, and other supplies may be helpful documents for government decision-makers, but they will not help contractors look good in a crowded market.

Recognizing this, government contractors and IT providers create powerful, immersive electronic experiences that help stakeholders and assist in decision-making. These activities can range from digital sites designed for web visitors to learn more about the company, some of which they can experience when visiting a physical office, to digital and physical advertising materials that offer company solutions and help training organizations better understand the challenges being addressed.

Review customer skills

No matter how big or famous a government contractor is, getting permission from an organization to talk about technical projects is often an impossible task. Understandably, organizations should be careful not to show awareness of those who provide material on the word or in the media. Instead, the entire government has new developers that run IT operations — these efforts need to be monitored. One way to create results is to look at the organization's leadership or the entire organization through rewards and opportunities to speak.

Several publications and organizations have annual programs highlighting good IT practices and leaders in governments, districts, and states. Organizations are often willing to share IT stories through rewards because they showcase innovations, can help improve performance and retention and don't realize they are marketers.

In addition to the promotional program, there are other benefits to developing media and awareness of public and local customer service. Non-governmental clients are often more willing to participate in social events, and attracting attention to the project may also demonstrate potential buyers in the Federation.

Create the events you want to sign

Contractors and IT providers are well aware that there is a need for more diversified marketing strategies to win corporate contracts than those that sell small businesses online on Dropbox or other similar "a-service" programs.

To some extent, there will be advertising campaigns aimed at reaching decision-makers from several military groups or other military entities - in some cases, on both sides.

These external activities may include liaison with commercial potential, job seals, or contract team expertise. But in the current market of competing companies, creating new and direct tasks to fulfil a contract or decision-maker to achieve a particular company can win the game and cause severe damage in the game-changer. Please make a difference between them.

More and more contractors continue to promote traditional advertising and advertising to meet other agreements but instead use commercial promotions and publishing services that may remain interested in often uncharacteristic work practices. Focus on organizational challenges, not on yourself

A significant shift in the work ethic and goal of state-owned IT media means that days of review or corporate reporting are a thing of the past. As a result, contractors and IT vendors need to be the developers of their communication skills.

Government IT journalists do not want to hear about marketing. They want to understand what is happening and the organizations' problems, and how contractors and IT providers find solutions to these problems. Once the problem is defined, the product/response message is provided randomly and avoids programs built around the answer to the search problem.

Expert Insight

Virtual assistant contractor tasks often entail producing PowerPoint presentations for conference speakers, developing brochures, and sending electronic newsletters. The Microsoft Office website offers free training in Microsoft Office products such as Word, PowerPoint, and Excel.

How to Become an Event Planner Intern

Event planners design and promote a wide range of events, both for business and pleasure. Corporate meetings or conferences, weddings, conventions, product unveilings, anniversary celebrations, and other events may be planned by them. Start as an intern with an event planning business or as an experienced freelance professional to get your foot in the door. This is a crucial first step in progressing in your profession and eventually opening your own event planning company.

1. Examine your abilities and passions. Event planners, according to the Bureau of Labor Statistics, require outstanding writing and vocal communication abilities. To properly negotiate contracts, you'll also need excellent mathematical and analytical skills. The ability to communicate in several languages, as well as the ability to

utilize banking and registration tools, is highly prized. Strong networking abilities are advantageous.

2. A bachelor's degree is required. Although a bachelor's degree is not necessarily necessary for interns, it substantially enhances your chances of being recruited in this area. However, you may be eligible for an internship while still in college. A degree in marketing, public relations, hotel management, or communications is an excellent place to start.

3. Learn how to arrange events at your school and in your community. To obtain relevant experience, volunteer your services. Plan events and meetings for campus groups and organizations. Don't expect to work as an event planner anytime soon. Working in areas of event planning where you are most comfortable and competent, such as treasury, promotion, decoration, or refreshments, is a good idea.

4. Internships with event planning firms are available. Prepare a strong cover letter and CV that details your previous job experience and education. When demonstrating your suitability for an internship position, be as precise as possible.

How Proposal Training Will Improve Overall Management

Proposal training teaches how to write proposals, find possibilities, and manage a strategy to stay profitable. Contractors and other project-oriented organizations can benefit from this training. Managers get expertise making critical judgments as a result of proposal training. Managers will learn how to interact with workers, higher-level company executives, clients, and partners with the help of good proposal training.

Recognize Opportunities

Proposal training enables company personnel to have a better understanding of the proposal process. Learning how to look for contract employment and recognize when new contracts become available is essential for this course. Managers that work with government contracts will find this very beneficial. Proposal training introduces managers to government websites, forums, and internet portals where new employment and possibilities may be found.

Making Proposals

Managers may be in charge of either developing their ideas or evaluating proposals that analysts and team members have set for them and other corporate executives. A crucial element of training is developing a good suggestion for large contracts and negotiations.

Recommending Projects

Managers will be better equipped to comprehend projects if they learn to detect proposal possibilities and produce excellent proposals. This allows them to make better decisions about which initiatives to support or suggest to their superiors. Even managers whose positions do not require them to write proposals might benefit from training since it allows them to analyze project proposals more effectively.

Dealing with Contractors

Managers who have been taught to draught and read proposals will spot flaws in the bids submitted by contractors. This strengthens the company's negotiating position, which frequently results in reduced prices, superior quality, and a better working relationship with the best contractor for the task.

Once your agreements are in place, the federal government may be a great business partner. However, getting to the stage where you're genuinely securing money takes time. Like some other national organizations, the federal Small Business Administration makes it plain on its website that the federal government is not in the business of awarding grants to establish or develop businesses. Instead, the government prefers to do business with little companies like yours. Federal contracts may be profitable, and many people like to give opportunities to small firms, particularly minority-owned enterprises.

1. Find out which federal agencies do business with your industry. Your product or service may have many federal contracts. Suppose your company is in the transportation industry, for example. In that case, you may discover that the Department of Commerce, the Environmental Protection Agency, and the Department of Defense all have open contracts to transport products or equipment.

2. Look for available contracts that pertain to your company in the federal internet databases. Contracts start and close every week so that you can find new possibilities every week.

3. For the contracts that interest you, follow the thorough application process. These generally entail providing detailed information about your company, successful projects or track record, financial position, and other criteria that an agency will use to assess whether or not you can and will provide the goods and services you claim.

4. Apply for specialized incentives that might help you meet federal contracting requirements. The Environmental Protection Agency, for example, offers grants to assist minority and women-owned firms in developing the resources needed to complete the EPA's goals and criteria. The award is intended to help a small, minority-owned

firm become a successful government contractor, and it must be used.

5. Apply for vendor status with the federal General Services Administration. When you become a GSA vendor, your company is added to a list of approved suppliers that any federal agency can utilize for standard requirements like office supplies, plumbing, minor repairs, and courier services at any time. You may also bid on government contracts more quickly since your business information is already on file with the federal government because you are GSA authorized.

6. Continue to follow up on contract bids with agency contacts and seek new contract possibilities. Because the government is sluggish, you'll have to play the odds and offer as many chances as you can if you want to start collecting government business money. You'll probably have to try a few times before you succeed.

Future opportunities

Martin: Rosa believes a new regulation adopted by the Small Business Administration in 2017 has a lot of promise. Contracts worth almost $100 billion a year will now be assessed against the SBA's small company goals. Small firms, which may lack the means or skills to work worldwide on their own, now have access to the whole globe.

"This allows small firms to learn how to do business on a global scale," she added.

"Having solid certifications and a willingness to apply them allows for expansion and the assurance of being paid in US dollars."

Why Seek Government Contracts for Small Businesses?

There are several reasons small firms pursue government contracts, and those who do not do so are undoubtedly missing out. Consider the following reasons why your small business should aggressively explore government contracting opportunities as part of its customer growth 1. The government is the largest customer in the world.

If you overlook the federal government's contracting opportunities, you're basically ignoring the single most significant source of new clients, with an annual contracting market valued between $350 billion and $500 billion.

Government contracts favor small businesses.

It is also the objective of the US government to give 23 percent of the $500 billion spent yearly on federal contracts to small companies.

That may not appear to be a huge number, but in what other bidding circumstances do you have any certainty that the prospect will choose your small business over a much larger one?

In the private sector, this is practically unheard of.

You may also utilise the Federal Procurement Data System to find out which federal departments haven't met the 23 percent goal. You will almost definitely be given preference over non-small company firms if you reply to an agency's request for proposals in this circumstance.

More data offers small firms an advantage.

Consider the latest proposal or offer you send to a potential client. How useful would it have been to know exactly what the customer was searching for and how much they were willing to pay when creating that bid and determining your rates?

It would completely alter the game. However, when it comes to government contracts for small enterprises, this fantasy may become a reality every time. Federal agencies are required by law to produce written budgets each year that specify precisely what they expect to buy and how much money they have set aside for it.

What's more, the best news for company owners is that. Those budgets may be seen on the Office of Management and Budget (OMB) website, which is open to the public. You may obtain the inside scoop on your prospective customer's strategy and goals for the contract you're proposing if you're prepared to dive in and conduct some research while you prepare your proposal.

www.ingramcontent.com/pod-product-compliance
Ingram Content Group UK Ltd.
Pitfield, Milton Keynes, MK11 3LW, UK
UKHW022220230426
12048UKWH00016BA/967